Ancient Egyptian Homes

Brenda Williams

Heinemann LIBRARY

www.heinemann.co.uk/library
Visit our website to find out more information about **Heinemann Library** books.

To order:
☎ Phone 44 (0) 1865 888066
▤ Send a fax to 44 (0) 1865 314091
▢ Visit the Heinemann Bookshop at www.heinemann.co.uk/library to browse our catalogue and order online.

First published in Great Britain by Heinemann Library, Halley Court, Jordan Hill, Oxford OX2 8EJ, part of Harcourt Education Ltd. Heinemann is a registered trademark of Harcourt Education Ltd.

© Harcourt Education Ltd 2002
First published in paperback in 2003
The moral right of the proprietor has been asserted.

Editorial: Nick Hunter and Jennifer Tubbs
Design: Jo Hinton-Malivoire and Tinstar Design (www.tinstar.co.uk)
Illustrations: Art Construction and Geoff Ward
Picture Research: Maria Joannou and Virginia Stroud-Lewis
Production: Viv Hichens

Originated by Ambassador Litho Ltd
Printed in China by Wing King Tong

ISBN 0 431 14581 4 (hardback)
06 05 04 03 02
10 9 8 7 6 5 4 3 2 1

ISBN 0 431 14586 5 (paperback)
06 05 04 03
10 9 8 7 6 5 4 3 2 1

British Library Cataloguing in Publication Data
Williams, Brenda
Ancient Egyptian Homes. – (People in the past)
640.9'32

Acknowledgements
The Publishers would like to thank the following for permission to reproduce photographs: AKG London p.**17**, /Erich Lessing pp. **8**, **24**, **26**, **29**; Ancient Art and Architecture Collection pp. **14**, **35**, **36**, **38**, **39**, /B. Norman p. **20**; Ashmolean Museum p. **40**; Committee of Egypt Exploration p. **32**; Philip Cooke/Magnet Harlequin pp.**5**, **13**; Peter Evans p. **42**; Manchester Museum pp. **21**, **43**; Werner Forman Archive pp. **7**, **10**, **12**, **16**, **22**, **28**, **30**, **34**, **41**.

Cover photograph of an ancient-Egyptian baker reproduced with permission of Werner Foreman Archive.

The publishers would like to thank Dr Christina Riggs for her assistance in the preparation of this book.

Every effort has been made to contact copyright holders of any material reproduced in this book. Any omissions will be rectified in subsequent printings if notice is given to the publishers.

Contents

Words appearing in the text in bold, **like this**, are explained in the Glossary.

Land of the Nile

The Egyptians created the first great **civilization** of the ancient world, a remarkable way of life that lasted about 3000 years. The ancient Egyptians were farmers, artists and builders, living in a land surrounded by the harsh deserts of North Africa.

The land of Egypt

Most of the land was hot and dry, as Egypt still is today. A narrow strip was made green by the waters of the River Nile, flowing north from the heart of Africa into the Mediterranean Sea. Every year the Nile flooded. When in flood the Nile was known as *Hapi*; out of flood it was called *Iteru*.

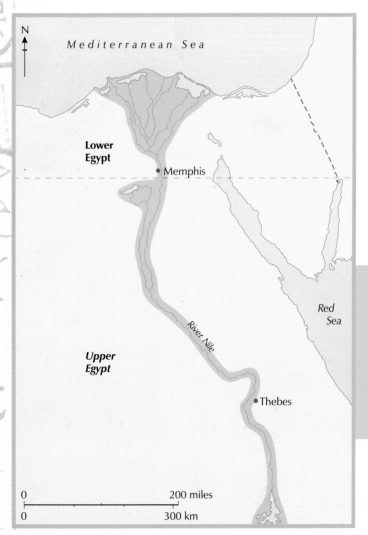

The rising waters spread black **fertile** soil along the riverbanks, enriching the fields where farmers grew food. From about 6000 years ago, people began to farm beside the Nile, building villages and towns.

This map shows the two parts of Egypt, Upper and Lower Egypt, and two of the most important cities. Egypt stretched along the River Nile, between areas of dry, hot desert.

This wall painting of craftsmen comes from the tomb of Rekhmire, an important official who served two rulers, Thutmose III and Amenhotep II. During his life Rekhmire was in charge of the workers shown on the wall of his tomb.

How do we know about the Egyptians?

The Egyptians left some of the most amazing **monuments** in the world. Visitors to Egypt still marvel at the stone temples, the pyramids and the tombs in the Valley of the Kings, where the Egyptians buried their rulers. The most famous tomb, found with most of its treasures still inside, is that of the boy-pharaoh Tutankhamen (a pharaoh is an Egyptian king). The workers who built these large tombs lived in special towns and built their own small tombs, too.

From these and other finds made by **archaeologists**, we know a little about ordinary Egyptians – about family life, clothes and food, furniture and decoration, and the homes people built. Paintings, carvings and writings also help tell the story of the Egyptians at home. This evidence helps us to recreate, in this book, the home lives of ancient Egyptians – from poor workers long forgotten, to the rulers whose statues and tombs we can still see today.

A very long history

A **priest** named Manetho wrote a history of Egypt. From such writings, **historians** have worked out that about 5000 years ago King Menes, ruler of Upper (southern) Egypt, conquered the northern kingdom of Lower Egypt. After him, 30 **dynasties** ruled, from the time of Menes until 332 BC when Egypt was conquered by Alexander the Great. In all that time, the homes in which Egyptian families lived changed as little as their everyday lives.

People of the flood

◄► ◄► ◄► ◄► ◄► ◄► ◄► ◄► ◄► ◄► ◄► ◄► ◄► ◄► ◄► ◄► ◄► ◄►

In Egypt, good land (land suitable for farming) was scarce, and good timber for building was even scarcer. Most Egyptians lived in villages, close to the River Nile. Fathers and their grown-up sons often lived side by side. New houses were often built on top of the crumbled mud-brick remains of old houses.

Watch the waters

Each year, as water poured downstream from the rain-soaked heart of Africa, the River Nile rose. The rising floodwaters, dark with mud, spilled over the riverbanks, leaving behind a thick, **fertile** silt. On this 'black land', or *Kemet*, the farmers of Egypt built their villages, planted fruit and vegetables, and herded cattle, goats and sheep. They dug canals with raised banks to carry water to the fields, beyond which stretched the hot, burning 'red land' or *Deshret* (desert).

Every house-builder wanted to be close to clean water, from a **well** or ditch, but also on high ground safe from flooding. After the Nile flood went down, people were busy re-marking fields, clearing out ditches and repairing walls and houses that had got wet.

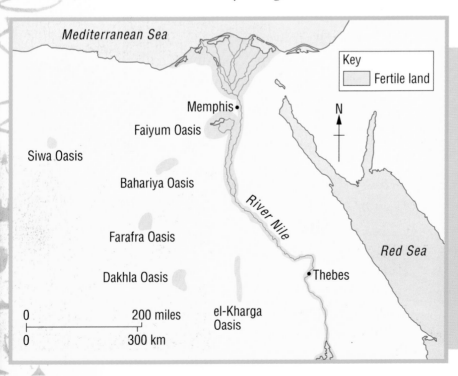

This map shows how the Egyptians settled along the River Nile. Their land was a green oasis over 1000 kilometres long. Beyond lay desert and the wide, wild outside world. The Nile gave Egypt its three seasons: Flood, Planting and Harvest.

An organized society

Ancient Egyptians preferred living together, in towns and villages. Some lived and worked in great cities, with huge temples to honour the gods and royal palaces, the homes of the king or pharaoh. The pharaoh was treated like a god. He owned all the land, and had absolute power over the army, navy, law courts, temples and trade.

Below the pharaoh were the **nobles**, who included his relatives, high officials and generals in the army. They had splendid homes, though not as big as the pharaoh's. Next came government officials, teachers, doctors, lawyers, **astronomers**, **architects**, **scribes** (writers of documents) and **priests**. At the bottom were the workers, soldiers, farmers and **slaves**, whose homes were often little better than mud and reed huts, but whose hard work kept Egypt going.

This 'Nilometer' was used to measure how high and fast the Nile's level rose. Records were kept every year so farmers knew roughly when to expect a good or bad harvest. It also showed people where it was safe to build homes, above the high water mark.

Towns and villages

The Egyptians were good at building and making things. They were especially clever at **geometry**, which they used for architecture and map-making. They were expert stonemasons, carpenters, metalworkers and jewellery-makers. They made skilful use of local building materials, such as reeds, palm trees and mud. They used their construction skills to build temples, tombs, palaces and forts, as well as houses. Painters and sculptors decorated walls of important buildings, such as tombs, with pictures of everyday life.

The Egyptian household

There was no official religious marriage ceremony in Egypt. Couples who set up house together were regarded as 'married'. Parents probably arranged marriages for their daughters, choosing suitable young men. If things did not work out, a couple could separate. If a husband died, his **widow** could marry again.

A home for the family

Most family homes were small and crowded. Ancient Egyptians loved children. Pictures show families at work and play, and written records mention some households by name. We learn of a man named Hekanakhte, whose household (meaning the people he was responsible for feeding) numbered sixteen, including his wife, mother, maidservant, daughters and sons – one son at least being married with his own family. However, we do not know if all these people lived in one house.

This painting comes from the tomb of Inkerhau. His wife is seated behind him and the children are made to look small and naked by the artist. The tomb is near Thebes. Wall paintings like this provide valuable information about the Egyptian household.

Children were loved and also useful. They were expected to help around the house, cooking and cleaning, fetching fuel and water. They also did their share of the work in the fields or workshops. In Egypt, children were expected to look after their parents in old age. Egyptians hoped for many children because, in spite of parents' care and their prayers to the gods, many babies died from diseases.

Living together

The 'extended' family included grown-up children, though many youngsters left home as teenagers to find work, or to marry. People often added new rooms on top of their houses, for extra space. Workers' houses, like those at Deir el-Medina, do not look big enough for more than six people, but they probably held about ten on average. Since people spent much of their time outdoors, they probably did not mind overcrowding at home. Privacy was a luxury enjoyed only by the rich.

Enjoying life

Although they worked hard, Egyptians did enjoy some leisure time. They had days out: a picnic at the tomb of their **ancestors**, or a boat trip on the Nile. Homeowners with gardens enjoyed relaxing beneath shady trees, and in the evening, many Egyptians liked to sit out on the flat roof of their home – chatting, singing, playing games or simply gazing at the moon and stars in the night sky.

Household pets

Family pets included cats and dogs. Cats were much admired for their independent natures, and there was a cat-goddess named Bast. Dogs are also shown in tomb paintings, sitting by their owners. Many cat **mummies** have been found, and a smaller number of dogs, sometimes buried in little **coffins**. Family cats went with people on bird-hunting trips to the Nile marshes. Cats also caught mice that crept in to raid the family's grain store.

Life in town

Towns were centres for trade and government. In the large cities, such as Thebes, enormous temples stood, which were the heart of busy farm and 'factory' work, such as cloth-making. The workers who ran the city lived in clusters of town houses. Streets were narrow and town houses were close together. If people needed extra living space, they usually built upwards.

The town house

Many town houses were two or three storeys high, with a small courtyard in front. Models of such houses have been found in tombs. Paintings in merchants' tombs show their town houses, with a workshop on the ground floor, living rooms in the middle, and grain stores on the roof. The smaller houses of poorer townsfolk had only one floor, with three rooms. More elegant homes had a terrace on the upper floor, from which the residents could take the air and see what was going on outside.

Egyptians placed small clay models of houses in the tombs of dead people. They are known as 'soul-houses'. This tall, narrow town house has small windows and a slit-like doorway to keep the house cool.

Keeping warm and cool

It was usually hot by day, but at night it often got very cold. On chilly nights, Egyptians burned **charcoal** in large pottery bowls to keep warm. Usually, keeping cool was their main concern. On hot nights many people slept out on the roof. Indoors, they had a form of air-conditioning, soaking mats in cold water to cool the hot air. Water stored in clay pots evaporated slowly, also cooling the room.

The house-owner used the ground floor for his business (perhaps as a workshop), while the family rooms were upstairs. Stairs led up to the flat roof, which was a good place to sleep on hot summer nights. People cooked food on the roof, and some families even kept cows and poultry on their rooftop. Few town houses had bathrooms. People fetched water from a **well**, and kept water in pottery jars on a stand in the courtyard.

Off to do a deal

From their houses, townspeople went to the market to do business. The ancient Egyptians did not use money, but exchanged goods instead. People traded whatever they had left over – cloth they had woven, fish they had caught or vegetables they had grown.

Most people made their own cloth, bread and clay pots. In the towns there lived skilled craftworkers who made jewellery, wooden furniture, and carved stone vases and cups. Metalworkers or smiths hammered lumps of **copper** into shape to make tools.

Neighbours

People in the same trade often lived next door to each other. From lists of workers, known as town rolls, we learn of **scribes**, copper-workers, sandalmakers and brewers all living as neighbours in the same street. So people always knew which part of town to go to when they wanted to buy something.

Workers' villages

On important building projects, workers lived together 'on site', in government-run villages. We know quite a lot about three such villages, at Deir el-Medina, Kahun and El-Amarna. At Deir el-Medina, the workers were building tombs in the Valley of the Kings, the burial place of the pharaohs.

Life at Deir el-Medina

The workers who lived at Deir el-Medina were better off than many ancient Egyptians. They were looked after by the state. Their village had a single main street, with houses on either side. Each house had three big rooms, a kitchen and a yard. People kept their food and other stores in underground cellars. Deir el-Medina was laid out more spaciously than another workers' settlement, at El-Amarna. Here narrow side streets led off the main street, and the houses were small and close together. Neither village had a **well**, so water had to be brought in by donkeys.

This is what Deir el-Medina looks like today. The houses here were made of mud brick, with plastered walls and flat roofs. The front door opened onto the street, and each house had a cooking area and yard at the back.

From the written records left by the officials, we know that after ten days' labour the workers at Deir el-Medina had two days of rest. Each morning they collected their metal tools from the site store, and handed them in again in the evening, under the watchful eye of a **scribe** who made sure none were stolen. Everyone took a break at midday.

Bosses and workers at Kahun

The village at Kahun was built for the workers building the pyramid of Sesostris. When the job was finished, they moved away and the houses were abandoned. Kahun was carefully planned in two parts separated by a wall. There was a wall all around the town, too.

In the eastern part of the town lived the bosses: officials, overseers (like foremen) and better-off workers. On the other side of the wall were the houses of the ordinary workers. There were over 200 homes made of mud-brick, whitewashed on the outside and some with as many as seven rooms. In the better-off district of Kahun there were more than ten 'executive mansions', with up to 70 rooms.

A carpenter at work. He is using a tool called an adze to trim a piece of wood. Egyptian carpenters fastened wood together using joints similar to those still used today, and made plywood with up to six different layers of wood glued together. They usually used wooden pegs instead of metal nails.

Houses of the poor

The earliest houses in Egypt, dating from around 7000 years ago, were small huts made from river **reeds**, sticks and mud. An early town found at Merimde Beni Salama, just north of modern Cairo, has a regular pattern of blocks and streets. It was built around 4700 BC, and perhaps as many as 16,000 people lived there. Most of the later towns studied by **archaeologists** are just as neatly laid out.

Mud and reeds

Stone and timber were too expensive for poor people, so they used materials that they could find by the river – reeds and mud. Some reed houses were probably very like those still lived in by some people in the Middle East today (see page 20). Other homes were made of mud-brick, or of a framework of sticks plastered over with mud (this method is known as 'wattle and daub'). There were also pit-houses, made by digging out a shallow pit, and roofing it over with branches.

A model of a house, with the flat roof typical of Egyptian houses. Egyptian houses had small windows, with bars or **shutters** to keep out the sun and dust. This is a small house, with a walled courtyard.

The homes of the poorest people were very small, about as big as one room in your house today. It must have been crowded, especially since many poor families shared their home with a goat, a goose or a couple of ducks!

The tomb-builders of Deir el-Medina were employed by the government. They were much better off. They even had women servants, who ground grain to make flour – a daily task because bread was the Egyptians' main food. Poor Egyptians did all their own housework: grinding grain, carrying water, fetching firewood and keeping the home tidy.

Inside a worker's house

The homes at Deir el-Medina (which were better than most workers' houses) measured about 5 metres by 15 metres, and into this area were fitted three or four rooms. From the street, people walked directly into the living room, where a palm tree post in the middle held up the roof.

Smaller rooms led off from the living room. At the back was the kitchen, which was part of the enclosed yard with a roof of tree branches to let out smoke and cooking smells. Here was the brick oven, for baking the daily bread. In the bedrooms, people slept on raised mud-brick platforms about 10 centimetres off the floor. In the walls were shallow niches, or recesses, in which families probably stood small statues of gods or other religious objects.

Homes for the wealthy

The ancient Egyptians liked living close together, and few people expected to have much privacy. Only the rich enjoyed spacious living, in homes that were much grander than the homes of farmers and tomb-builders.

The ruling class

Government officials, **scribes** and army officers lived in large houses inside walled courtyards. Their homes were like farm-estates, producing food and other essential items for everyday life. Within the walls were grain stores, sheds for cattle, a bakery and a brewery for making beer – a favourite drink in Egypt. Big houses also had a **weaving** shed, where workers made **linen** cloth, and a carpenter's workshop, for making wooden furniture, tools and even **chariots**.

This painting shows a scribe called Nakht and his wife in the garden of their house. The house is shown to the right (with its roof vents for cooling air to flow in). The garden pond (left) is surrounded by trees. Nakht and his wife are shown worshipping the god Osiris (centre).

A comfortable home

A rich Egyptian's house was cool and comfortable. It had an open courtyard, with a colonnade (walkway with pillars). This must have been a pleasant place to entertain visitors or relax with friends, cooling off in the northerly breeze that brought relief from the scorching heat. Most wealthy Egyptians also loved their gardens, where a pool and trees gave the cool shade that they loved so much.

The house was square, with a central living room, and other rooms grouped around it. The house provided rooms for the owner, his wife, children, relatives and servants. The owner also needed stables for his chariot-horses, cellars for wine and storerooms for food.

The private family rooms were kept for the women and children, and for sleeping at night. One room was for visitors, where the man of the house would entertain friends. In the 'working area', servants prepared food and drink, ground grain, baked bread and wove linen cloth for clothes.

In this wall painting from the tomb of Nebamun, servants wait on dinner guests sitting on elegant chairs. Heaps of food can be seen to the left of the painting. In the lower scene, women wear wigs topped with cones of scented fat or wax. As the room grew warm, the cones melted and released trickles of sweet-smelling perfume to cool the guests.

No urban transport problems

One of the oldest city plans in existence shows a drawing of Thebes, the city the Egyptians called Nowe. From such plans, we can see how close together they lived. Almost everyone walked everywhere. There were no traffic jams in Egyptian towns, because there was no traffic, except perhaps on market days when the donkey-caravans came to town.

The royal household

The pharaoh lived in a palace. In fact, Egypt's ruler had several palaces, since he was always on the move, visiting temples and checking all was well in his country. The Egyptian royal family was often large, since kings with more than one wife might have many children. Pharaoh Ramses II claimed to have more than 100 children by his numerous wives.

Managing the royal household was rather like running a top-grade hotel. Soldiers, officials, servants and relatives all travelled with the pharaoh.

The royal family at home

The grandest buildings in Egypt were temples, built for the gods out of stone. Palaces, known in Egypt as 'great houses' were made of mud bricks like workers' houses, but were much larger. Few of them lasted very long. Only in one or two, like that at Malkata built for Amenhotep III in the early 1300s BC, can we still see the decorations on walls, floors and ceilings. The king's bedroom had flying vultures painted on its ceiling. This was a symbol of the pharaoh.

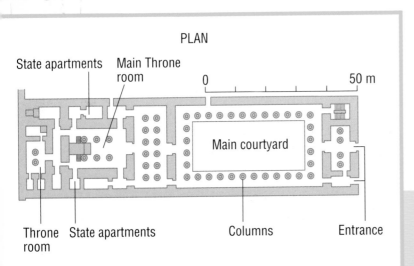

PLAN

State apartments   Main Throne room

0   50 m

Main courtyard

Throne room   State apartments   Columns   Entrance

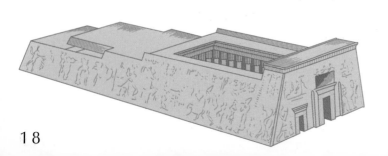

This is what the royal palace of Merneptah at Memphis probably looked like. Pharaoh Merneptah was the son of Ramses II and, like his father, a successful soldier. The ground plan shows the large courtyard, with columns around its edges, leading to the throne rooms and private apartments.

The royal family lived in comfort. Their palace rooms were decorated with soft colours and painted scenes of animals and plants. Blank walls had painted windows facing walls with real windows, because Egyptians liked both sides of a room to be in balance.

The life of a pharaoh
The pharaoh had daily religious duties to perform, appearing in public most days, and attending to the running of the kingdom. He walked every day through a guarded doorway from his private rooms into the throne room, where he sat in state on a raised platform of **alabaster**. Amenhotep's queen, Tiy, had her own suite, and so did his daughter. The palace also had quarters for other relatives and wives, and hundreds of female attendants. There were also royal officials, most importantly the **vizier**, the chancellor, the steward, the generals and lots of servants.

Servants washed the dusty hands and feet of visitors, and served food and drink. They also waved fans to circulate air inside the palace to keep it cool. Royal children played with the children of court officials and **nobles**, who had their own houses near to the palace.

What were homes made of?

An Egyptian liked to keep cool in the heat of the day, but keep warm at night, when the temperature could drop sharply. Keeping out rain was not a problem as it hardly ever rained, so mud was a perfectly suitable material for building. It was cheap, plentiful and easy to use. From the Nile, the Egyptians also had an endless supply of **papyrus** and other **reeds**. Reeds tied in bundles were often used instead of wood.

Reed homes and mud bricks

Some homes were made almost entirely of reeds, as some homes in southern Iraq still are today. Others were made from mud-bricks. To make bricks, builders mixed mud, straw and sand with water.

Dried mud-brick can last a surprisingly long time: there are ancient mud-brick tombs in Egypt over 5000 years old. Mud-bricks were easy to knock down when you wanted to, and so Egyptians often pulled down old mud-brick homes and built new ones on top of the rubble. They seldom bothered with foundations, though they did dig out cellars for storage. Roofs were flat, and often a builder would leave side walls sticking up, ready to add a new room on top of the home if it was needed.

Reed houses are still built today by the Marsh Arabs, a people who live in southern Iraq. The homes are sheltered by palms and are next to the river.

Walls, doors and floors

Walls were between 40 and 125 centimetres thick, with palm stems or wood added for extra strength. Occasionally stones from disused temples or a local quarry might be used for walls. Doorways were made of stone too, with wooden lintels (the bit over the door). Windowsills were also sometimes made of wood. Doors were made of wood, and had locks with keys. Inside, walls were coated with plaster made from limestone powder and water, and then painted. Floors were made of earth, trodden so it became rock-hard.

Windows and air-vents

An Egyptian house had small windows, without glass but with bars and **shutters**. Windows were set high in the walls, to keep out the glare of the sun and dust from the street. Vents on the roof, shaped like scoops, sucked in the cool north wind to freshen the air inside the house. The west wind blew in hot air and sand from the desert, so no one in Egypt wanted a house with windows facing west.

Builders' tools found at Kahun. To make bricks, the Egyptians poured wet mud and straw into brick-shaped wooden moulds. They lifted off the mould, then left the brick to bake hard in the sun for two or three days.

Brick by brick

Experts can sometimes work out the age of an Egyptian building from the size of its mud-bricks. Different sizes were used at different times in Egypt's history. The builders used wet clay as mortar to cement the bricks together.

Furniture

◀▶ ◀▶ ◀▶ ◀▶ ◀▶ ◀▶ ◀▶ ◀▶ ◀▶ ◀▶ ◀▶ ◀▶ ◀▶ ◀▶ ◀▶ ◀▶ ◀▶

To modern eyes, most rooms in an ancient-Egyptian house would have looked rather bare. There was not much furniture. Wooden furniture was hard to make, because local tree-wood was tough and knotty. Furniture-makers often had to fix small pieces of wood together, so chairs and beds were expensive.

The finest Egyptian furniture is very elegant, carved and gilded (gold-covered). Some examples have been found in tombs such as Tutankhamen's. We can assume that poor people had very little furniture, other than what they made themselves.

Stools, chairs and tables

Most people either sat on the floor, or on low stools. The best stools had upward-sweeping corners and woven or leather seats, with a padded cushion on top. Only rich Egyptians owned chairs, made of small pieces of wood glued and pinned together. They were either painted, or coated with a mixture of chalk and glue.

Egyptian bedroom furniture like this would have belonged to wealthy families. This furniture was found in the tomb of Hetep-heres I, the chief queen of Pharaoh Sneferu at Giza. At the far end of the bed is a headrest. Only a rich person could afford a chair like the one shown here.

Night lights

Many people went to bed when it got dark, tired after their long working day. As night fell, families lit candles made from tallow (animal fat), or oil lamps made of clay with a wick of rag or reed. The finest lamps were made from paper-thin **alabaster**, so thin the soft light shone through. Lamps were often placed on lamp stands.

Layers of thin wood were added to furniture for decorative effect. Some tables had a single leg. Others had three or four legs. They were made of wood or wicker (woven twigs of a bendy tree such as willow). Egyptians did not often use tables, but instead placed trays or jars of wine and water on stands. Clay was used to make pottery jars, basins and plates. Water-jars stood by the front door, for guests to help themselves to a drink.

Beds and chests

Poor people slept on the floor or on mud-brick platforms softened with feather-filled cushions or a mat woven from **reeds**. Only rich people slept in beds. At one end of the bed was a footboard. At the other, instead of using pillows, Egyptians rested their necks on wooden headrests, which look rather uncomfortable!

People were buried with furniture to use in the **afterlife**. In Tutankhamen's tomb there were stools, chairs (one small enough for a child to sit on), footstools, chests and beds, including a folding camp bed.

Family valuables and clothes were usually stored in boxes or chests. These were fastened with wooden locks or cords.

Decoration

◀▶ ◀▶ ◀▶ ◀▶ ◀▶ ◀▶ ◀▶ ◀▶ ◀▶ ◀▶ ◀▶ ◀▶ ◀▶ ◀▶ ◀▶ ◀▶ ◀▶ ◀▶

The outside walls of houses in ancient Egypt were painted white, to reflect the sun's rays and so keep the house cool. Inside walls were painted, sometimes boldly, in colours. Some workers' houses had a band of brown paint around the wall at floor level, then stripes of red, black and white. Above that was a pale, sandy colour.

The walls of Tutankhamen's burial chamber were painted with scenes of the young pharaoh entering the **afterlife**. The north wall shows Tutankhamen being welcomed by the god Osiris and the goddess Nut, while at the right the pharaoh's successor Ay wears a leopard-skin robe to perform the sacred ceremony known as 'The Opening of the Mouth' on the dead ruler's mummy. The baboons on the other wall represent the hours of night – twelve were painted. On the floor is Tutankhamen's gold coffin.

Household hints

With no fitted carpets or thick curtains, the Egyptian house must have been quite easy to keep clean – apart from all the dust and sand that blew in. People were house-proud, and some useful household tips were written down on papyrus. One says: 'To get rid of mice, spread fat from a dead cat everywhere you don't want the mice to run. To stop a snake coming into the house and disturbing you at night, stop up its hole with an onion.'

Palaces and large houses were decorated with bright patterns and colourful pictures of plants, birds, fish, and tables laden with food were painted on their walls and ceilings. Wooden columns in a big house were carved and painted with lotus and other flowers. In the private rooms, wall paintings showed the family at play, or hunting birds in the marshes. Splashes of paint still visible in a room in the Pharaoh Akhenaten's palace suggest that it may have been used as a play room, where his children were free to do their own decorating!

Floor coverings

Rich people could afford expensive floor tiles, painted in bright colours. However, in most houses people simply put down woven mats made of **reed** or animal skins over the dirt floor. People also used reed mats as partitions, to wall off part of a room for privacy (perhaps if someone was ill).

Stone trees

One of the most important trees in Egypt was the date palm. From ancient times house builders used palm stalks covered in clay to make pillars – this was cheaper than paying for expensive imported timber, shipped in from Syria and Lebanon. Pillars were used to hold up roofs of porches or terraces. If date palm stalks were scarce, river reeds (**papyrus**) tied into bundles were used instead. When the wet clay dried, the pillar looked as good as stone. Later **architects** copied these reed-columns, for decoration, but made them of real stone.

Entistaining

The ancient Egyptians were fond of a good time, and both rich and poor people enjoyed a party. The poor drank beer, which they brewed themselves, while the rich drank wine, often imported from foreign countries. It was apparently no disgrace to get drunk. One painting shows a lady guest being encouraged to drink more by a servant, and cheerfully saying that she doesn't mind at all if she drinks too much!

A banquet

An Egyptian banquet, prepared for a rich family, would have been a glittering occasion. The soft light of oil lamps playing on the fine furniture, the soft **linen** dresses of the women and the wonderful gold and silver jewellery worn by both men and women must have been a wonderful sight. The room would be filled with the scent of flowers, arranged on the table for decoration, and with the perfumes from the guests' headdresses.

Egyptians must have enjoyed music, since musicians are often shown in paintings. Here three women play instruments: a harp (left), an instrument that looks like a cross between a violin and a guitar, and (right) an instrument that may be a drum. Drums, flutes and pipes were also played to accompany songs and dances.

Silent music

We do not know what ancient Egyptian music was like, because none of it was written down until Greek-Roman times. In 2001 **archaeologists** found what may be the words of a love song written on a tomb, and we have pictures of musicians and a few instruments themselves, some still playable. So we know what sounds they made, but not the kinds of tunes the Egyptians would have played on them.

The ideal meal, according to a prayer for the dead, was bread, beer, beef and roast goose. From paintings in tombs, it is clear that rich Egyptians often sat down to a good many more dishes, with vegetables such as peas, beans, lettuce and cucumber (and onion and garlic, which they believed prevented illness). Most Egyptians ate squatting on the floor, but at an elegant dinner party, the guests sat on chairs and stools. They ate with their fingers, using knives to cut the food into small portions, and washed their greasy fingers in water poured from jugs by servants.

Entertainers sing and dance

Musicians entertained the diners, on harps, lyres (stringed instruments), flutes and small drums. The harp player might be asked to sing traditional songs, some of them hundreds of years old. After the music, a pair of singers might sing love songs, while girls danced, wearing very little apart from **loincloths** and beads.

An evening's entertainment might also include a magician, a performing ape or acrobats. When it was time to go home, servants lit the way with flaming torches as the guests thanked their hosts and departed into the starry night. Indoors, oil lamps would be blown out, the master and mistress retired to bed, and the servants at last were able to go to sleep.

Private lives

Most poor ancient Egyptians were too busy to have much of a private life. From the clues in wall paintings and tomb-finds, we have glimpses of parents playing with children, of husbands and wives, of family outings and quiet moments at home.

Women's lives

At home, men and women shared many simple pleasures – chatting, listening to music, playing with the children (perhaps a board game such as Senet), sitting in the garden, dining with friends. In many ways, women in ancient Egypt had more freedom than women in ancient Greece, where women mostly lived secluded lives.

Clothing at home

People liked to keep cool indoors. Their clothing was made from a material called **linen**, made from the fibres of the **flax** plant. Poor women wore unbleached cloth, and richer ladies liked dresses bleached white or dyed orange, yellow or green. The ancient Egyptians did not like wool (it was too hot and scratchy), and farmers did not grow cotton in Egypt until much later times.

Here we see a man and his wife making offerings to the gods. Her dress is so fine it is transparent. Tomb paintings show an idealized world, yet they are our best visual clues to the private lives of Egyptians.

At home, men wore a linen **loincloth** or a short **kilt**, sometimes with a long overskirt or shirt-like tunic. Women wore ankle-length dresses. Evidence of what ancient Egyptians wore comes mostly from pictures and from lists of clothes sent to the **laundry**. Clothes put into tombs soon rotted, leaving only scraps of material which tell us little about what people wore.

Dressmaking and hairdressing

Women made clothes at home, and repaired and patched old clothes many times. A simple dress was made by folding a rectangle of cloth, sewing up the sides (leaving holes for the arms) and cutting a hole in the fold for the head.

A maidservant would help a rich woman to do her hair. Egyptian women wore their hair long, with ribbons, bands and scarves to keep it in place and free of dust. Both men and women also wore **wigs**, made from human hair, and false hairpieces. Both sexes also wore make-up. Children are pictured with shaven heads, and a lock of hair hanging down on one side.

This Egyptian make-up box contains jars in which people kept cosmetic oils and powders. Egyptians particularly liked to outline their eyes in black and green.

Working in the household

Poor people did their own housework and shopping, though privileged workers such as the tomb-builders of Deir el-Medina had servants to help. Servants did the heavy tasks: carrying water, grinding grain, washing clothes in the river, cleaning the house and carting away toilet waste. An important domestic job was **weaving**, done by the women in the family and by servants.

Off to market

Food had to be provided fresh every day, from the fields or the market. When ancient Egyptians went shopping, they took something to exchange, such as a basket of dates, a clay pot, a bunch of onions or a fish caught that morning. At the local market, shoppers would stroll around, looking at the rugs, sandals, beads, loaves of bread, rolls of cloth, jars of **cosmetics**, vegetables, tools and other items on display. Stalls selling fruit and beer did a lively trade refreshing the traders in the heat of the market.

This wooden figure of a servant girl was made in about 1900 BC, to go inside her master's tomb. On her head she carries a basket filled with bread and pieces of meat.

Days off

Workers had time off for religious festivals. There were more than 60 holidays each year. Workers who failed to turn up for work had to give a reason to the **scribe**, who often wrote it down. That is how we know that Egyptians took days off for birthdays, funerals or because there was 'trouble at home' – sickness or a family argument.

A tomb picture at Saqqarah shows men with shopping bags slung across their chests. Thieves were chased by market wardens who, from the evidence of one picture, used trained baboons as 'police dogs'. The baboon is shown biting a thief on the leg!

A fair deal

Although Egyptians did not use coins, an agreed standard weight of **copper**, called a *deben*, was a useful guide to a fair deal. For example, a pig was worth 7 *debens* of copper. So to buy a pig, a household had either to hand over that amount of copper, or an assortment of goods – a pig was worth about two goats or five pairs of sandals. To make a **coffin**, a carpenter would ask for around 20 *debens* of copper (or three pigs).

Egyptians paid their taxes in goods as well. A farmer had to hand over part of his harvest. If he refused, he was marched away to do forced labour. The tax collector accepted whatever people had. So often he went away satisfied with baskets of grain, coils of rope, mats, goats, cattle or a couple of pigeons!

Clean and healthy

Ancient Egyptians were very clean at home. Most people washed themselves, and their clothes, in the river or in the nearest **irrigation** ditch. They kept a basin of water indoors for washing. Only rich people had bathrooms with piped water, flowing through stone or clay pipes (**copper** pipes seem only to have been used in temples). Most people carried their water in pots from public **wells** or from the river. Water from a well was raised by a simple machine called a *shaduf* (a weighted pole with a bucket on one end), and poured into a pond.

Washing and waste

In the bathroom was a slab of stone, with a drainhole, like a shower-tray. The bather took a shower by standing or lying on the stone, while a servant tipped water over him.

Priests washed several times a day, and temples were spotlessly clean. Houses were kept sweet smelling with pots of flowers and perfumes. People who could afford to would send their dirty washing to the local **laundry**.

This is an Egyptian toilet seat. Made of limestone, it probably belonged to a rich homeowner. Most people used wooden seats, or made do with pottery bowls or a hole dug in the sand.

A recipe for hair-growth

Many pictures show Egyptian men with shaven heads, and we know men wore **wigs**. Yet some men obviously worried about losing their hair. This unusual mixture was for making hair grow: 'Paws of a dog, one part; kernel of dates, one part; hoof of a donkey, one part. Cook very thoroughly in a pot and rub into the head.'

Toilet arrangements were fairly basic, because water was too precious to waste and there were no drains for houses. In a rich person's house, the toilet was usually a wooden or limestone seat resting on mud-brick supports above a sandbox or clay pot. A servant emptied it out. Poorer people might have just a stool with a hole cut in it. The toilet waste was taken away and either tipped into a ditch (which was not very hygienic), or used as manure on the fields.

Household rubbish, including food remains, was either buried or dumped on a tip, where **scavenging** animals such as vultures and jackals soon ate most of it.

Looking good, keeping well

Men were clean-shaven. They shaved their beards (and heads) with razors made of **bronze**. Rich women spent a lot of time bathing and rubbing their skin with oils and perfumes. Eye make-up helped to protect people from sunburn and eye infections.

If people got ill at home, they had to go to the temple to see a doctor, and paid for treatment with food, drink or other goods. Medicines were made from plants. For example, a doctor put willow leaves, which contain aspirin, on wounds to reduce swelling and ease pain. If someone broke an arm or leg at home or work, the doctor set it with a plaster cast made from a mixture of flour and cream.

In the kitchen

Men servants did most of the cooking in the kitchen of a great house. Poor women cooked for their own families. Tomb pictures mostly show the lives of rich families, so we see servants baking bread and brewing beer. The kitchen was at the back of the house, and the oven for baking, heated by a fire of **charcoal** (charred wood), wood or animal dung, was in the yard. People also cooked food on the roofs of their houses, which was cooler and meant the living rooms were free from smoke and cooking smells.

Bread, cakes and honey

Bread was the basic food for all ancient Egyptians. From the worn teeth of mummies, it's clear that the bread most people ate was full of grit, from coarse flour. Bakers made at least fifteen kinds of bread and various cakes. A popular cake called *shat* was made from dates and honey, and baked in the shape of a triangle. Honey was used to sweeten many foods, and the Egyptians kept bees in long tube-hives laid in rows on the ground. When they wanted to collect the honey, they lit fires to smoke out the bees.

An Egyptian cook is modelled in clay fanning his fire to make it burn. He holds some duck in his left hand which he is about to cook. Kitchen scenes in tombs show people grinding grain, carrying sacks of flour, sieving the flour to remove lumps and mixing dough to make bread.

This painting from the tomb of the scribe Nakht shows a harvest offering. A man and woman bring fresh food and plants to add to the feast, which includes grapes, fish, birds, vegetables and fruit. The water and **fertile** soil provided by the Nile meant that most years few people went hungry.

Meat and vegetables

Firewood was scarce. Charcoal was the main fuel for cooking. It made a hot fire with little smoke. Meat was roasted over a brazier of charcoal, just like a barbecue. Smaller pieces of meat and fish were cooked over fires of dry **reed** stems. The meat of cattle, goat and sheep were all eaten, but roast goose was a particular treat. Meat was a luxury, however, and few poor people ate it very often. Their daily meal was usually bread and onions, and perhaps a fish caught from the river.

Temple lists tell us about the foods people brought to the temples as offerings to the gods. Some tombs contain the remains of food, left for the dead person to eat in the **afterlife**. In their farms and gardens, the Egyptians grew dates, figs, onions, cucumbers, radishes, beans and lettuces. Oil for cooking and lighting came from the moringa or drumstick tree and the **flax** plant (linseed oil), and later from olive trees. Grapes were grown to make wine, and barley bread was **fermented** to make beer.

Gardens

◁▷ ◁▷ ◁▷ ◁▷ ◁▷ ◁▷ ◁▷ ◁▷ ◁▷ ◁▷ ◁▷ ◁▷ ◁▷ ◁▷ ◁▷ ◁▷ ◁▷

'May my soul rest on the branches of the trees which I planted.'
So reads an **inscription** in an Egyptian tomb of around 1400 BC.
The ancient Egyptians loved gardens. Some gardens were like
botanical parks, with rare trees and exotic animals brought from
foreign lands.

Tomb paintings of gardens include every detail. Here we see the fruit
trees and date palms from the side, while the pond is shown from
above, so the painter can include the fish and ducks swimming in it.
A woman in the top right corner gathers and stores fruit from the trees.

36

Painted gardens

Egyptians liked painted flowers as much as the real plants in their gardens. The sweet-smelling blue lotus is shown in lots of wall paintings. They expected to spend eternity surrounded by leafy vines, palms and fig trees, believing that a shady tree was one of the first things they would see in the world of the dead.

Trees for fruit and shade

Tomb paintings show gardens with date palms, fruit trees and pools with ducks and fish. Trees were valued for their fruit, and for the shade of their leaves. The Egyptians planted sycamores (more like figs than European sycamores), figs, pomegranates and many varieties of nut trees, along with willows, acacias and tamarisks. They also grew grapes and other kinds of trailing vines.

Gardens were a useful source of food, providing fresh vegetables on the doorstep for town dwellers. Poor people may have sown seeds in baskets or pots, to grow fresh salads and flowers. The Egyptians loved flowers indoors, in their hair and painted on their walls. Pictures show chrysanthemums, cornflowers, roses, irises, jasmine, narcissi, vines and poppies, with **papyrus** and lotus growing wherever there was water.

The gardener

The big house of a rich man had a large garden cared for by servants. A wall surrounded the garden. This was to stop animals from the farmyard wandering in and nibbling the plants, and also to provide privacy for the owner and his family.

Watering delicate plants in such a hot country must have been a problem, especially if the gardeners had to look after plants brought from a cooler climate. Pictures show gardeners using a *shaduf* to pour water from an **irrigation** ditch into channels to carry water around the garden, just as the farmers used this simple machine to raise water onto their crops.

Religion at home

Religion was extremely important in ancient Egyptian life. Each village and town was protected by a god. The Egyptians had many gods and goddesses. The most important were Re the sun god, Horus the sky god, and his parents, Osiris the god of the dead and Isis.

Household gods

The earliest people of Egypt worshipped animal and nature gods. Later Egyptian gods were often shown in art with animal bodies, or looking like humans with animal heads. Many people probably involved these gods in their home lives.

The Egyptians built temples for their gods, and put statues of the gods inside. **Priests** washed and dressed the god-statue every day, and offered it prayers and gifts of food. Ordinary people said their prayers at home, where they kept small god-statues. In the workers' homes at Deir el-Medina, the first room held a small **shrine** for the household god.

Protecting the home

Three favourite household gods were Bes the dancing dwarf, Taweret goddess of childbirth and Hathor goddess of **fertility**. They were thought to protect people from harmful evil spirits, ward off sickness and bring healthy babies.

A figure of the dwarf god Bes glazed to make him shiny. Egyptians thought he was a jolly little chap, who would banish all evil demons from their homes. They prayed to him for aid with childbirth, and to protect their children from harm.

When Pharaoh Thutmose III died about 1426 BC, Egyptians believed in at least 740 gods! We know because their names are listed in his tomb. Egyptian religion was not gloomy, and a song from the Middle Kingdom sums up their view of life. 'Make a holiday,' it says, 'for no one who departs this life ever comes back again'.

Grinning Bes looked fierce, with his lion's mane, horns and knife, but this was only to scare off demons. He was pictured on beds, headrests, chairs and even mirror handles. Taweret (part hippo, part crocodile and part lion) was equally ferocious-looking, and she too had a knife to deal with unwelcome spirits.

At home, people probably made offerings of food, flowers and oil to the images of their protector-gods. The images would carry the **hieroglyph** sign meaning 'protection'. When setting up home, probably one of the first things a couple did was to set up an **altar**, where offerings and prayers would be made. Childless couples would set up tiny fertility figures, in the hope that these would help them have a baby.

The mummy of a cat. Many Egyptian gods were pictured with animal heads, and some animals were especially highly regarded. Temples were given over to worship of the cat-goddess Bast.

Homes of the dead

The ancient Egyptians believed there was an **afterlife**, to which human souls went after death. Every person was supposed to have a twin shadow, or *ka*. If a dead body decayed, the *ka* would have no body to return to, and could no longer exist. That is why the Egyptians preserved the bodies of the dead, by making **mummies**.

Tomb preparations

Egyptians built tombs to last many lifetimes. At Deir el-Medina, the workers built their own tombs, which remained undisturbed until the AD 1800s. These 'homes of the dead' were dug from the rock above the village. Little rooms were built, with vaulted ceilings, and on the walls the village artists painted lifelike scenes. The cone-shaped tombs are small-scale copies of the pyramid tombs of the great pharaohs of old.

Making a mummy

When someone died, the Egyptians tried to keep the body looking as lifelike as possible. It took 70 days for the body of the boy-pharaoh Tutankhamen to be mummified. The **embalmers** removed vital organs (brain, stomach, liver and intestines). The body was treated with salts, and packed with linen, sawdust or dry **lichen**. After being rubbed with lotions and oils, it was wrapped in **linen** bandages.

Clay models of houses were put in tombs, for the souls of the dead to inhabit in the afterlife. These soul-houses give us a good idea of what the ordinary Egyptian house looked like.

The mummy was put in a wooden **coffin**. It was taken to the tomb and stood upright by the door while the funeral took place, including a ceremony known as The Opening of the Mouth, to restore life to the dead.

A new world

Inside the tomb, **mourners** placed food, clothes, tools, furniture and treasured objects that the dead person might need in the next world. They also placed inside small model houses, 'houses for the soul', and little figures, some holding tools ready for work.

Tomb paintings describe the jobs a dead person did, events in his life, and also show his family. One tomb at Deir el-Medina, that of a worker named Sennedjem, contains wall-pictures showing his mummy being treated by the embalmer. Other pictures show Sennedjem with his wife Iyneferti and family, worshipping the gods. In the world beyond death, he is shown ploughing the fields, reaping a harvest and looking after an orchard of trees weighed down with luscious fruit. The green world of death was very different from the hot and dusty reality of life for most ancient Egyptians.

The decoration on the lid of this casket shows Tutankhamen and his queen in a garden. They enjoy the garden while their servants pick mandrake plants below them. The ancient Egyptians looked forward to an afterlife in which they would enjoy other gardens, and other homes, in the company of those they loved. To them, heaven was a shady garden.

Goodbye to the earthly home

At a funeral, women mourners made as if to cling on to the coffin, while the coffin-bearers struggled to take it into the tomb. There was no doubt who would win. As a song put it: 'No one may linger in the land of Egypt'. Even a pharaoh had to leave the earthly home.

Buried history

Ancient Egyptian towns, tombs and **monuments** have been studied by **archaeologists**. The most famous monuments, such as the pyramids, were built as tombs for great pharaohs. The homes of ordinary people soon crumbled into dust.

Peering into the past

To find out about everyday ordinary life, and ordinary homes, we need to look at the few sites where traces of workers' homes remain. Three important sites are the town of Kahun (built near the pyramid of Sesostris II), the workers' village near El-Amarna built by Pharaoh Akhenaten, and the village of Deir el-Medina on the west bank of the Nile at Thebes.

The finds there help us understand a little more about how ordinary Egyptians lived. The 'pyramid-town' of Kahun was discovered by the British archaeologist Flinders Petrie. Pottery and **copper** tools were found in the remains of the houses. Other finds included balls of thread, fishing nets, wooden hoes and rakes, dolls, games-boards and writings on **papyrus** pages (one on veterinary medicine, some on maths, others with legal letters and accounts). Lists of household servants and wills were also found, which show how Egyptians left property to their wives when they died.

At Kahun, workers building a royal pyramid lived in a town built specially for them. They hauled stones and made bricks, working in eight-week shifts for as long as the Nile flood prevented them from working their fields. They were paid in grain and beer, and lived in rows of mud-brick houses. Maybe the pharaoh visited from time to time, to see how work was getting on, and stayed in the biggest house in town.

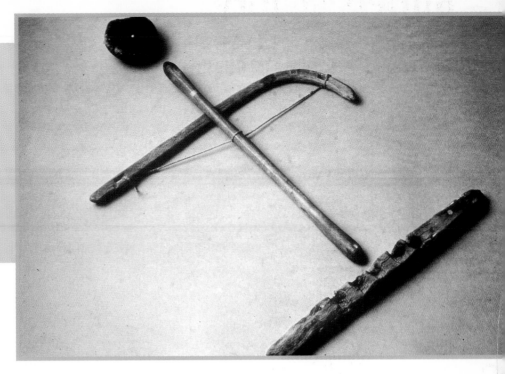

A bow drill used by workers at Kahun. The drill bit is held in by the bowstring, and by 'bowing' the drill backwards and forwards the workers made a hole.

Tomb finds

Most royal tombs were robbed long ago, and are now empty. Later pharaohs were buried in rock tombs in the Valley of the Kings. In this desert valley the tomb of the boy-pharaoh Tutankhamen was found still intact in AD 1922. Tutankhamen's tomb, modest by ancient Egyptian standards, contained more furniture and treasures than any other Egyptian tomb opened by archaeologists. The Egyptians buried all kinds of things in the tombs of their dead, giving us a glimpse into their long-gone world.

Pictures and writings

Other evidence about Egyptian homes and families comes from wall paintings inside tombs, temples and palaces. These show ordinary Egyptians at work and at play. We can also read writings by Egyptians themselves, such everyday jottings as **laundry** lists, taxmen's records and letters.

All this evidence helps to tell the story of the ancient Egyptians at home, and to make them seem more alive, more like us, despite the 5000 years that separate our times.

Timeline

All dates are BC. Pharaoh's dates refer to reigns.
All dates are approximate as they vary from source to source.

4700
Egyptians are already building towns

About 3000
King Menes, the first pharaoh, rules all Egypt

2575 to 2130 Old Kingdom
Imhotep builds the first pyramid at Saqqarah for Pharaoh Zoser.
Pharaoh Khufu builds the Great Pyramid at Giza.

1938 to 1600 Middle Kingdom
First schools in Egypt

About 1895
Workers' town of Kahun is built during reign of Sesostris II

About 1981
Building starts on royal palace at Malkata in Thebes for Amenhotep III

1539 to 1075 New Kingdom
The period of Egypt's greatest power and wealth. Workers' village of
Deir el-Medina is built.

1353 to 1336
Reign of Akhenaten, who tries to start a new religion

1333 to 1323
The boy-pharaoh Tutankhamen rules Egypt

About 1250
Temples at Abu Simbel built during reign of Ramses II

332
Egypt is conquered by Alexander the Great, who makes Alexandria
the capital. After this the Ptolemies, Greek kings, rule Egypt.

69 to 30
Life of Cleopatra, Queen of Egypt. After her death, Egypt is ruled
by Rome.

Sources and further reading

◄► ◄► ◄► ◄► ◄► ◄► ◄► ◄► ◄► ◄► ◄► ◄► ◄► ◄► ◄► ◄► ◄► ◄►

Sources

Ancient Egypt: The Land and Its Legacy, T.G.H. James
(British Museum Publications, 1988)

Daughters of Isis: Women of Ancient Egypt, Joyce Tyldesley
(Viking, 1994)

Discovering Ancient Egypt, Rosalie David
(Michael O'Mara, 1993)

Myths and Legends of Egypt, Lewis Spence
(Studio Editions, 1994)

Technology in the Time of Ancient Egypt, Judith Crosher
(Wayland, 1997)

The British Museum Book of Ancient Egypt, eds. Quirke and Spencer
(British Museum Press, 1992)

The Splendour that was Egypt, Margaret Murray
(Sidgwick and Jackson, 1979)

Women in Ancient Egypt, Gay Robins
(British Museum Press, 1993)

Further reading

How Would You Survive as an Ancient Egyptian? Jacqueline Morley
(Franklin Watts, 1999)

Legacies from Ancient Egypt, Anita Ganeri
(Belitha, 1999)

The Egyptians, Rosemary Rees
(Heinemann, 1994)

The Life and World of Tutankhamen, Brian Williams
(Heinemann Library, 2002)

Visiting the Past: The Pyramids, Haydn Middleon
(Heinemann Library, 2002)

Glossary

afterlife world of the dead

alabaster Egyptian alabaster was a mineral, a form of limestone, used for making decorative objects

altar place for making offerings to a god or goddess

ancestors grandparents, great-grandparents and so on

archaeologist person who finds out about the past by looking for the remains of buildings and other objects, often beneath the ground

architect someone who designs buildings

astronomer scientist who studies the stars and planets

audience chamber room in which a ruler receives visitors to listen to their requests

bronze metal made by mixing melted copper and tin, used in ancient times for tools and weapons

charcoal wood heated in a slow fire inside a dirt mound, so that it chars (goes dry and black)

chariot light cart with two wheels, pulled by horses

civilization society with its own rules, and an advanced way of life

coffin box in which the body of a dead person is put

copper soft metal used by ancient peoples to make tools

cosmetics make-up; creams, paints, or scents used to make a person look, feel or smell nice

dynasty ruling family. The first Egyptian historian Manetho listed 30 dynasties of kings

embalmer person who preserves a dead body, as a mummy

fermented process to make beer and wine is called fermentation

fertility/fertile ability to reproduce, ground that is fertile grows good crops

flax plant whose fibres are used to make linen cloth

geometry mathematics to do with shapes and angles

hieroglyphics Egyptian picture-writing; the name means 'sacred writing' in Greek

historian someone who studies the past from writings, and writes about ancient peoples

inscription writing cut into stone or some other hard material

irrigation watering plants in fields by ditches and other artificial means

kilt garment that is like a skirt

laundry place where workers wash dirty clothes

lichen small dry plant growing on rocks and trees, as soft as moss

linen cloth made from the woven fibres of the flax plant

loincloth simple wrap-around garment worn like underpants

monument building or statue built to remind people of a famous person or a famous event

mourners people grieving over a dead person, at a funeral and afterwards

mummy body of a dead person specially treated to stop it decaying

noble person of very high social rank

papyrus reed growing in Egypt, with many uses, including paper for writing on

priest person with special religious duties; in Egypt priests looked after temples

reed tall plant growing beside rivers and lakes

scavenging scavengers are animals which feed on rubbish and dead matter

scribe person trained to write; in Egypt scribes wrote government records and wrote letters for other people

shaduf simple machine for lifting water, a see-saw pole with a weight at one end and a bucket at the other

shrine specially holy place, or a container with doors, inside which a god's statue or a king's coffin was kept

shutters small door-like flaps over a window

slave person who has to work for an owner, and has no personal freedom

vizier chief official, rather like a modern prime minister

weaving intertwining of fibres to make cloth or rugs and mats

well hole dug to get at underground water

widow a woman whose husband has died

wig artificial hair

Index